The WRIGHT BROTHERS
Take Flight

written by **Nel Yomtov**
illustrated **by Daniele Dickmann**

a Capstone company — publishers for children

The author wishes to dedicate this book to his granddaughters, Jamie Shea and Nina Raye.

Raintree is an imprint of Capstone Global Library Limited, a company incorporated in England and Wales having its registered office at 264 Banbury Road, Oxford, OX2 7DY – Registered company number: 6695582

www.raintree.co.uk
myorders@raintree.co.uk

Copyright © 2025 Capstone Global Library Limited
The moral rights of the proprietor have been asserted.

All rights reserved. No part of this publication may be reproduced in any form or by any means (including photocopying or storing it in any medium by electronic means and whether or not transiently or incidentally to some other use of this publication) without the written permission of the copyright owner, except in accordance with the provisions of the Copyright, Designs and Patents Act 1988 or under the terms of a licence issued by the Copyright Licensing Agency, 5th Floor, Shackleton House, 4 Battle Bridge Lane, London SE1 2HX (www.cla.co.uk). Applications for the copyright owner's written permission should be addressed to the publisher.

Editorial credits
Edited by Christopher Harbo
Designed by Tracy Davies
Production by Katy LaVigne
Printed and bound in India
Design Element: Shutterstock/kzww

Direct quotations appear in bold italicized text on the following pages: Page 7 from Wilbur Wright's 30 May 1899, letter to the Smithsonian Institution, General Correspondence: Smithsonian Institution, 1899–1909 (loc.gov, 4 January 2024).

978 1 3982 5832 7

British Library Cataloguing in Publication Data
A full catalogue record for this book is available from the British Library.

All product and company names are trademarks™ or registered® trademarks of their respective holders.

All the internet addresses (URLs) given in this book were valid at the time of going to press. However, due to the dynamic nature of the internet, some addresses may have changed, or sites may have changed or ceased to exist since publication. While the author and publisher regret any inconvenience this may cause readers, no responsibility for any such changes can be accepted by either the author or the publisher.

Contents

Chapter 1
The brothers Wright 4

Chapter 2
An idea takes flight 8

Chapter 3
Making history at Kitty Hawk 14

Chapter 4
Pioneers of the age of flight 24

More about the Wright brothers 28
Glossary 30
Find out more 31
About the author 32
About the illustrator 32

Chapter 1 *The brothers Wright*

Wilbur Wright was born in April 1867. His brother, Orville, was born in 1871. The boys grew up in a pleasant two-storey home in Dayton, Ohio, USA.

Their father was a bishop at a local church. Their mother encouraged the boys' interest in tinkering with mechanical things.

Orville

Wilbur

Orville was friendly and outgoing. He had a good business sense and sold kites he'd built to his friends.

Thanks, Orville. We can't wait to fly it.

Wilbur was very intelligent and an outstanding gymnast and American football player.

Business boomed. The brothers began designing and building their own line of bicycles.

They wrote and published a newsletter aimed at cyclists. The paper advertised their bicycle business.

The brothers moved their Dayton bicycle shop six times. Along the way, they even built some of the machinery needed to make their bikes.

Chapter 2 *An idea takes flight*

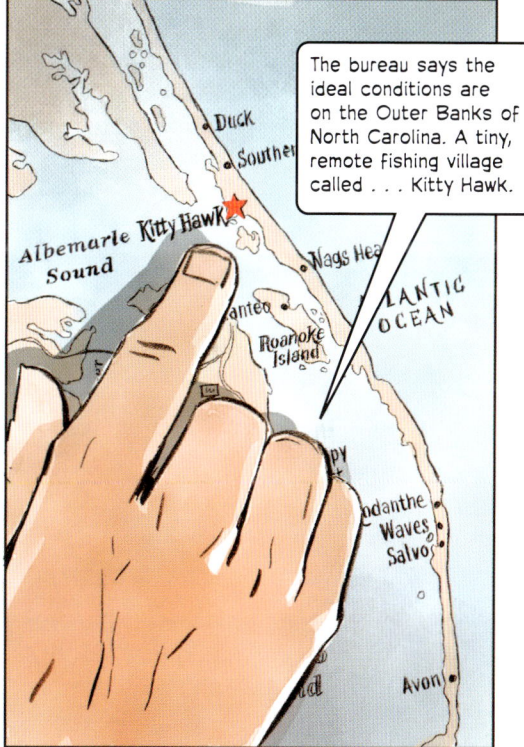

Chapter 3 *Making history at Kitty Hawk*

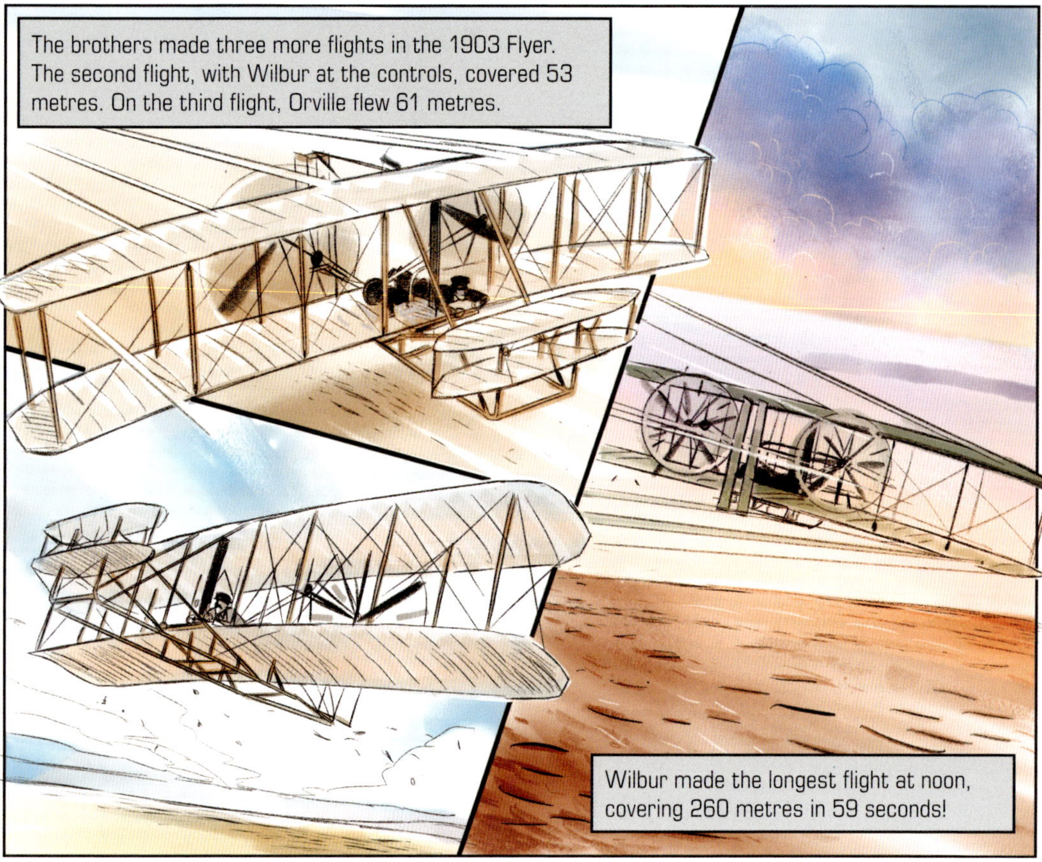

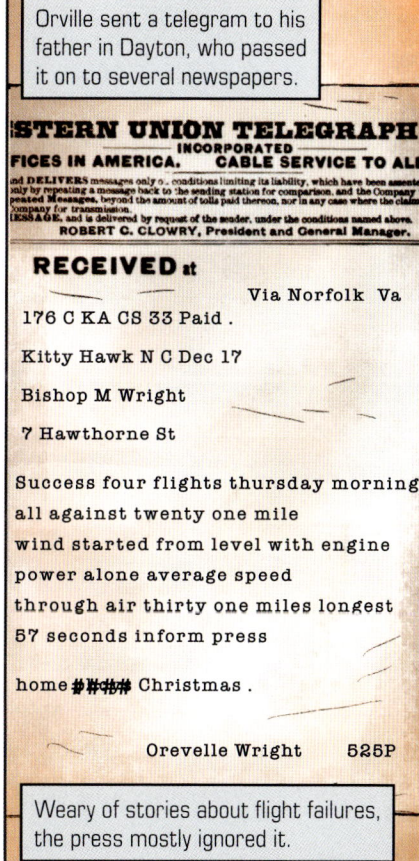

Chapter 4 *Pioneers of the age of flight*

The brothers made it back home for Christmas...

We've got to prove to the world that our machine has practical uses.

Then we'll build a new Flyer with a stronger body and a more powerful motor.

In the spring of 1904, the Wrights built their Flyer II. Their new testing ground was a cow pasture outside Dayton.

In the spring of 1905, the brothers completed Flyer III. In October, Wilbur set a flying record by staying in the air for 39 minutes and covering 40 kilometres.

Wilbur wowed audiences in France with more than 100 flights. Orville successfully demonstrated a Model A for the US Army.

The brothers agreed to make planes and train pilots for the French government and the US Army.

As the year passed, the brothers put on flying demonstrations in Germany and Italy. In late September 1909, Wilbur made a 20-mile (32-km) flight around New York City.

In November, the brothers formed the Wright Company to build and sell planes. The two men had become famous worldwide – and had won their place in history.

Inspired by the Wrights, aviation technology developed rapidly. In 1927, Charles Lindbergh completed the first solo non-stop flight across the Atlantic Ocean.

By the 1950s, jet airliners that carried hundreds of passengers flew to places around the world.

In 1969 – only 66 years after the Wrights flew at Kitty Hawk – US astronauts flew all the way to the Moon.

Today, powerful rockets carry vehicles to Mars to explore the planet's surface.

And all of it was made possible by Orville and Wilbur Wright. Two brothers who opened the skies to fulfil humanity's desire to explore the heavens and beyond.

MORE ABOUT THE WRIGHT BROTHERS

- The Wrights built hundreds of bicycles between 1896 and 1904. Only five are known to still exist. The model held at the National Museum of the US Air Force in Dayton, Ohio, is the only known example of a woman's bike built by the Wrights.

- The Wright Brothers earned worldwide fame but did not become wealthy. Their money was used up by a series of lawsuits they filed to protect the patents they held on their inventions. The patents would have prevented others from making, using or selling the ideas and works they created.

- The first passenger death in an aeroplane happened on 17 September 1908. During a flight demonstration for US Army officials, Orville Wright took up Lieutenant Thomas Selfridge as his passenger. In the flight over Fort Myer, Virginia, the Flyer's propeller hit a wire that held the aircraft's two wings together. The Flyer crashed to the ground, killing Selfridge and badly injuring Wright.

- American-born Madame Hart O. Berg was the first woman to fly anywhere in the world. On 7 October 1908, Wilbur Wright took her on a short flight in a Model A over the military campground at Camp d'Auvours in France. Berg was a supporter of the brothers' efforts and worked hard to convince the French government to buy planes from them.

- Wilbur Wright died in 1912 at the age of 45 at the Wright family home in Ohio. Younger brother Orville died in 1948 at age 76. John Daniels, the man who took the photo of the brothers' famous first flight, died the day after Orville.

- In 1928, Orville shipped the repaired 1903 Flyer to a museum in London because he was upset by the unfair treatment the brothers received from the Smithsonian Institute. The Smithsonian had funded Samuel Langley's experiments but ignored the Wrights' breakthroughs. The Flyer was sent back to the Smithsonian after Orville's death in 1948. It is currently on display at the National Air and Space Museum in Washington DC.

- A small swatch of fabric from the 1903 Wright Flyer is on Mars. The swatch made the 482,805,000-kilometre journey to the Red Planet on NASA's experimental Martian helicopter in 2021.

- The Wright Brothers National Memorial is located in Kill Devil Hills, North Carolina – the area of the 1903 flights. The site is open to visitors and features a replica of the camp buildings and hangar used by the Wrights and a massive stone monument dedicated to the brothers.

GLOSSARY

aviation science of building and flying aircraft

bishop senior priest in the Roman Catholic, Anglican and Orthodox churches

conquest act of conquering

demonstration act of showing other people how to do something or use something

descend move from a higher place to a lower place

dolly small platform on wheels used for moving heavy objects

engineer someone trained to design and build machines, vehicles, bridges, roads or other structures

glider lightweight aircraft that flies by floating and rising on air currents instead of by engine power

humanity all human beings

mechanical having to do with machines or tools

patent legal document giving the inventor of an item the sole rights to make or sell it

propeller rotating blade that moves a vehicle through water or air

replica exact copy of something; some replicas are made on a smaller or larger scale than the original item

secretary head of a government department

shutter part of a camera that opens and closes to expose film to light when a photograph is taken

telegram message sent electronically over wires by a device called a telegraph

tinker repair or make small adjustments to something to see what will work

FIND OUT MORE

Books

The Big Book of Planes, DK (DK Children, 2020)

The Wright Brothers (Mini Movers and Shakers), Mary Nhin (Grow Grit Press, 2021)

Up in the Air: A Horrible History of Flight (Horrible Histories), Terry Deary (Scholastic, 2021)

Websites

kids.kiddle.co/Wright_brothers
Read more about the Wright brothers on this website.

www.bbc.co.uk/bitesize/articles/zdcskmn
Learn about the history of flight with BBC Bitesize.

www.youtube.com/watch?v=iKdQDX2OEpw
This video shows you more about the history of flight.

ABOUT THE AUTHOR

Nel Yomtov is an award-winning author of children's non-fiction books and graphic novels. He specializes in writing about history, current events, biography, architecture and military history. He has written numerous graphic novels, including *Raising the Flag on Iwo Jima*, *School Strike for Climate* and *Cher Ami: Heroic Carrier Pigeon of World War I*. In 2020, he self-published *Baseball 100*, an illustrated book featuring the 100 greatest players in baseball history. Nel lives in New York City, USA.

Author photo by Nancy Golden

ABOUT THE ILLUSTRATOR

Daniele Dickmann is a freelance artist born and raised in Rome, Italy. He graduated from the IED (Europe Institute of Design), where he's now a professor. His career began as a visual and storyboard artist for advertising companies and film productions. Daniele has since gone on to work for many publishing houses, illustrating historical series and fiction tales for young readers.

Illustrator photo by Daniele Dickmann